Hushes

The Ache Between Our Silences

Shubham Lohakare

BookLeaf Publishing

India | USA | UK

Made with ❤ on the BookLeaf Publishing Platform
www.bookleafpub.in
www.bookleafpub.com

Dedication

For the one who taught me what love could feel like.

This book is about you — brutally, honestly, entirely.
For the memories, the laughter, the silences, and the ache.
I am proud that I loved you enough for it to become poetry.

Preface

This book isn't a timeline.
It's a constellation —
of late-night kisses, cartoons on hostel beds,
Star Wars marathons, and unsaid goodbyes.

These poems weren't written to remember.
They were written because I never forgot.

Some are soft. Some ache. Some laugh mid-line.
They all began in rooms we once walked through,
in food we shared,
in moments that felt like forever — even if they weren't.

So if you're reading this —
thank you for being part of the kind of love
that's impossible to write down,
but I tried anyway.

Acknowledgements

To the people who held space for me while I held onto memories — Thank You!!

To my friends who listened, who read early drafts, who sat beside me while I cried, or simply let me talk about her without interruption — you have no idea how much that meant.

To the late nights, hostel corridors, unfinished conversations, and quietly unforgettable moments — thank you for becoming poetry before I even knew I was writing.

To the version of me who lived these memories, and the version who had the courage to revisit them — I'm proud of both of you.

And finally, to the one these poems are about —
You may never read this, but you gave me something worth writing down.
And that, in itself, is everything.

1. I Think I Have Stopped

The room that echoed of Euphoria,
Now attacks me with its tapestried walls.
The painted cartoons still spawn a joke.
Without your giggles,
I think I have stopped laughing a little.

The Lego models look at me unforgivingly,
Of being completed and unplayed
Who to breathe worlds into them with?
Without your words of reverie,
I think I have stopped dreaming a little.

The blankets have stopped smelling like you,
I no longer wake to your voice
Nobody corrects my wrong tune anymore.
Since your vows lost into the ether,
I think I have stopped loving a little

Every idle moment your memories haunt me,
Of the false hopes, of unfulfilled promises.
That unfinished movie teases me.
Since your last embrace,
I think I have stopped living a little.

2. Sunshine in a Frock

With frostings over the upper lip
Her smell lingered
Like a warm summer day.

Her amber frock, her white sandals
And the golden rays
That danced in play.

The birds would sing, as she walked
With each of her step
matched to their tune.

Her glistening eyes
Like the cool moonlight
A solace in the burning June

Her smile could power, a million Lighthouses
Her bouncy hair-strands
Plotting the schemes

There she was,
With her Ice-cream cone
An angel straight out of the dreams

3. Robbed

I saw you once — and that was that,
The world went quiet, smooth, and flat.
My thoughts, once mine, began to roam,
And somehow, all of them were yours alone.

You didn't speak, yet still I heard
A world began without a word.
No warning shot, no plan, no plea—
Just you, and then no more of me.

My thoughts, once neat, now ran unchecked,
Each corner of my mind, you had wrecked.
I tried to read, to sleep, to eat—
But you returned in every beat.

My nights replayed what wasn't yet,
Your name a song I couldn't forget.
I'd see your face in in-between,
Where waking ends and dreams begin.

You took it all — the calm, the thread,
The peace I had inside my head.
You've robbed me soft, without a crime.
And I've been yours since that first time.

4. The Moment Before

It was past midnight, quiet and bare,
The corridor hummed with hostel air.
You sat with worry stitched in tight,
Tomorrow's weight, too loud for night.

I brought your favourite, wrapped in foil,
A peace offering after the day's toil.
You didn't eat, just looked right through
Then laid your head where silence grew.

Your head on my lap, no need to speak,
The world unspooled, soft and weak.
A single bulb, a ticking fan,
And time forgot its clever plan.

You looked up once, then looked away,
Your lips moved slow, unsure what to say.
My hand just brushed against your hair—
Something old, familiar, rare.

There was a pause — not long, not loud,
Just enough to hush the crowd.
The kind of moment Mosby swore,
Deserved a drumroll right before.

And then it happened, barely planned,
No sudden move, no bold command.
Just breath and breath and lips that met—
The kind of moment hearts don't forget.

And now, whenever silence stays,
Or night drifts in its quiet haze,
My mind goes back to that hallway floor—
That kiss, that pause, that open door.

5. It Felt Like Love

You held my hand, And walked with me,
So I'd never drift like a lost decree,
And it felt like shelter in a storm.

You pulled me close, And held me tight,
Promised to never leave my sight,
And it felt like comfort, true and warm.

You made me laugh, You shaped my dreams,
Taught me to swim against the streams,
And it felt like blessings from above.

We shared the loudest laughter,
And hummed a tune both bright and shy,
You twirled with me as years flew by,
And it felt a lot like love.

6. Benaras

We left by bus with restless plans,
Two window seats and folded hands—
Returned by train, still sun on our tans.

Her hair was dark with streaks of hue,
The TC stared, unsure what to do—
"Which country are you from? Both of you?"

We sipped what locals swore was sweet,
And stumbled giddy through the heat,
Benaras danced beneath our feet.

The oar cut slow through water's skin,
You spoke of stars, and touched my chin—
The boat forgot which side was wind.

We chased old doors in painted rows,
Found secret ghats where no one goes,
And took soft pictures no one knows.

At Kashi's gate, we stood in line,
You nudged my arm to match your spine,
And let the incense blur the shrine.

The river roared in fire and sound,
The lamps rose high, the drums would pound,
But all I saw was you — spellbound.

7. Snowball

I used to cross the street in fear
if any dog was drawing near.
Not hatred, really — more mistrust,
Too loud, too fast, too quick to thrust.

You didn't push, you didn't preach,
You let the fear stay out of reach.
Just sent me memes at 1 a.m.—
Dogs in hats, cats stuck in hems.

I laughed, I liked, I saved a few,
And didn't say they changed my view.
Then came biscuits from the store,
You handed me a pack—nothing more.

We crouched beside the hostel gate
and watched the strays investigate.
You tossed some treats, and I just froze,
Still stiff from instincts I didn't chose.

When dogs passed by along our path,
I'd pull you close and do the math—
Just place you firmly up ahead,
My shield from what I thought I dread.

You'd roll your eyes, pretend to groan,
But always let me hide behind your tone.

One day you said, "Come, they've just been born,"
and led me out one quiet morn.
No box, no fence, just open ground—
a bundle barely making sound.

You picked one up, then took my hand,
Placed him in it like you'd planned.
"This one's Snowball," you softly said—
And I forgot the things I'd dread.

He smelled like milk and earth and sleep,
A tiny warmth I got to keep.
He barely stirred, just let me hold—
And something in me lost its cold.

We went again when new ones came,
Each day with puppies felt the same.
At first I watched, then knelt, then stayed,
And found my fear began to fade.

No speeches made, no lines you drew,
No "told you so," just something true.
Another tail, another grin—
Another way to let love in.

8. How We Kept Warm

We never said much about the chill,
The windows fogged, the air stood still.
The floor was cold, the light was low,
But love found ways to softly grow.

You wore that sweater, soft and wide,
With bear-ear flaps you wore with pride.
I'd say, "Turn them on," you'd lift them straight—
You, in those ears, made winter great.

We chased down soup like it was gold,
Warm in our tummies, and warmer to hold.
You'd steal my spoon with that sly grin,
And somehow always let me win.

Back in our room, the heater dead,
We'd order food, curl up in bed.
South Park played, ignored halfway,
As limbs and laughter slipped away.

One blanket shared, too small, too thin,
But perfect once we both crawled in.
Your feet found mine, your breath found space
To fill the corners of that place.

There was no need for grand displays,
Just jokes and food and quiet days.
A show we loved, a song half-played—
A home in all the mess we made.

And in that room, the cold outside
Would knock, but never get inside.
For love was there in every form—
That's how we lived, That's how we kept warm.

9. Without a Cue

It started with jokes too dark to share,
But you laughed first, so I didn't care.
A glance exchanged, a quiet spark,
Two twisted minds lighting up the dark.

Then came the dramas we both adored,
Stories and scripts we never ignored.
You'd quote a line, I'd jump right in—
The act began, and we'd always win.

In your room, we'd set the stage,
Improvised like we owned the page.
A scene would start with just one line,
The rest would fall in perfect time.

No script, no lights, no need to try—
Just one raised brow, one knowing sigh.
We played it out with voice and grin,
And somehow always knew the end.

In childhood tales, we found the thread,
Of lonely games and books we'd read.
We shared the wounds we never named,
And found our pasts were just the same.

We'd draw on scraps, paint midnight skies,
Write poems laced with stupid lies.
You'd start a thought, I'd write the rest—
Like somehow, you could read my chest.

We'd cram for tests the night before,
But end up on the hostel floor—
Singing songs we both half-knew,
Finishing lines before they were through.

A Shah Rukh line, a whispered song,
You'd say the start—I'd sing along.
No second guess, no need to try,
Just perfect rhythm, you and I.

They say soulmates are rare to find—
Two mirrored hearts, one tangled mind.
But we just laughed and called it fate,
Two weirdos who could create.

10. No One Saw Us Dance

It was 2:30, cold and still,
The kind of night that bites with chill.
We'd had some drink, just enough to glow,
And wandered out with nowhere to go.

The campus slept, no soul around,
Just mist and silence on the ground.
We walked without a place to be,
Your jokes, your hand, your eyes on me.

You wrapped my hoodie and laughed out loud,
I mocked your style, you took a bow.
Then half a verse escaped your lips—
Qaafirana, in quiet slips.

We kept on walking, soft and slow,
No plan, no rush, no need to know.
Then near the football field we stood,
You looked at me—I understood.

You kissed me soft, like we were mid-song,
Like stopping there just felt not wrong.
No drama, lines, or big reveal,
Just something quiet, close, and real.

You kept on humming, note by note,
That song half-sung in half a coat.
And then we danced—no beat, no plan,
Just fog and us, hand wrapped in hand.

My arms were loose, your breath was white,
We stumbled once, but held on tight.
No lights, no phones, no world in sight—
Just you and me and the campus night.

11. Almost Late

The morning crept in soft and slow,
But neither of us wished to go.

Your leg on mine, our breath aligned,
The world outside we'd left behind.

You would sigh low and find my chest,
I'd kiss your hair and hold the rest.

The sun would crawl across your hair,
And settle warm on skin laid bare.

A kiss, a smile, a quiet hush,
Before the corridor would rush.

Outside the noise, a hostel shout,
Inside — just us, not yet thrown out.

You'd press your lips just under mine,
And breathe me in like morning shine.

We'd talk of skipping class again,
Then scramble into clothes, still warm within.

12. Same Story, Different Screens

We weren't in the same place,
not even close on maps,
but still you felt one call away—
in memes, in rants, in apps.

Five, six FaceTime calls a day—
no reason, just to see
if your cat filter looked the same,
or if you still missed me.

We talked about the sky, the news,
the dreams we had, the lunch we chose.
You'd call me names too cute to say,
I'd act annoyed—then smile, I suppose.

We'd draw a comic, pick a theme,
no rules, just lines and little jokes.
And somehow, every single time,
we'd land the same exact strokes.

We'd screen-share shows at 1 a.m.,
syncing scenes we'd seen before.
You'd pause to rant, I'd mute to laugh—

it never once felt like a chore.

We talked for hours about our days,
and all the things we'd do when near—
the places, jokes, the quiet cafés,
the way your voice would sound right here.

We weren't in one place, that's true,
but every day, you were my part—
in every call, in every frame,
in every beat between my heart.

13. Lucknow

Ours wasn't the Lucknow of history books—
It was parks too wide to see in a day,
where we'd walk without needing a reason,
pause to take photos under arching trees,
or talk about nothing
until it became something we'd always remember.

It was chikankari shops tucked in old lanes,
where you'd pick kurtas and I'd pretend
to understand fabric,
just to watch you light up at a perfect find.

It was a café no one talked about,
that served rectangular pizza
like it had something to prove,
and a PlayStation in the corner
where we took turns being Spider-Man,
swinging through make-believe
while your head leaned on my shoulder
between levels.

It was cold—
the kind that seeped into bones,
and still we'd take autos out

to that Fauji Dhaba on the edge of the city,
where the Dal steamed against the night
and food arrived like a promise
you could actually eat.

It was summer—
hot, breathless,
skin sticking to cab seats,
and we'd still show up to the mall,
not to shop
but to wander the Home Centre aisle,
run our fingers across plates and spoons,
and whisper about our future kitchen
like we already lived there.

It was late-night movies
where we stayed for the credits,
even when the AC was too cold
and your nose went red.
It was holding hands and our super weird rhymes,
sharing popcorn,
and the quiet joy of doing nothing
but doing it together.

Some places stay, not for their skies,
but for who we were in those endless nights.

We were completely, wildly ours—
and that's what makes it hurt just right.

14. If She Had Been

If she had been the fire,
And I had been the ember glow,
She'd kiss the night in golden flickers,
And I would breathe where she would go.

If she had been the wind,
And I had been the echo,
She'd weave her voice through valley deep,
And I would sing the notes she'd know.

If she had been the water,
And I had been the mist,
She'd flow in rivers deep and wide,
And I would rise where she was kissed

If she had been Earth,
And I had been the meadow,
She'd toss the sun upon my back,
And I'd laugh in her shadow.

But she is the heart, unburdened, alive,
And I, the lingering ache left behind.
Once, I echoed in her every pulse,
Now, I am the silence she won't find.

15. What Love is Not

Love is not
a footnote in your therapy journal,
not a case study
in your spiral-bound mind.

It's not a voice note dissected
with three friends and a podcast.
Not a quiz result.
Not an attachment style.
Not a checklist of green flags
ticking themselves into approval.

It is not
the space between your texts,
not the silence you diagnose as avoidant,
not the overthinking
masquerading as awareness.
Love is not a game of who knows more
about wounds and triggers.

It is not
your Excel sheet of red flags,
the flowchart of "what he really meant,"
or the quote you repost

to justify your exit.

Love is not
the polished language of healing,
not your curated self on dating apps,
not your Instagram reel
of spiritual soundbites.

It is not
safe all the time.
It is not tidy.
It is not immune to mess.

And love—
for the love of God—
is not a lab rat
under your microscope.

It doesn't ask
to be decoded,
it begs to be felt.

So no,
love is not
what you learned from textbooks,
or therapists,
or late-night rabbit holes.

It is not a skill
you can hack.
It is not
a trophy
for the most "healed" heart.

Love is not a concept
you master.
It's a mystery
you keep missing
while you're busy
trying to name it.

16. Don't You Remember

Don't you remember
how we found each other
halfway between two cities
and made a world inside a weekend?

Those tiny studios we called home—
fairy lights, stone counters,
mirrors too big for the room.
We booked them like rituals,
promised each other
"Next time, one with a better view."

Don't you remember
the list of films we kept
in voice notes and late night texts?
We watched them all,
backs against velvet cushions,
your feet tucked beneath my thighs,
my hand on your shoulder
like it had always belonged there.

We played tourist with a plan.
Our maps came from
Bollywood wives and streaming dreams.

That one rooftop with pink sofas,
those cocktails that tasted like drama,
the overpriced cheesecake
you said was still worth it.

Don't you remember
Marine Drive?
How we walked without walking fast,
talked without needing to explain.
The sea didn't rush us.
It just listened.
Like I wish you would now.

I still carry
the echo of your laugh
in the back of a rickshaw.
The crease of your dress
on that Airbnb couch.

Your eyes lit by the projector glow
as credits rolled
and we didn't want to move.

So if you've left it all behind,
if those moments
don't tug at you the way they do me—
that's okay.

But I hope, just once,
when you visit that city again—
when the skyline flickers through a cab window,
or the sea wind brushes your face at Marine Drive—
you'll pause.
And you'll remember, too.

17. When We Finally Go

We learned to use chopsticks
with trembling hands and soy-stained lips,
laughing when rice slipped off the edge
and cheering at our tiny wins.

Sushi became its own love language—
shared plates, wasabi dares,
you stealing the last salmon roll
like it was written in our vows.

We'd send each other reels at night—
kawaii cafés with floating bears,
places that served noodles by train,
a bookstore lit like a Ghibli dream.

We had a list:
ramen in alleyways,
matcha in Kyoto,
kimonos in spring,
lunch under the cherry blossoms
with nowhere to be but here.

We said we'd visit Kasukabe—
not for temples or food,

but because we owed it
to a cartoon boy with thick eyebrows
who somehow shaped our childhoods.

It was never just Japan.
It was Japan with you.
The "let's go" whispered
between mouthfuls of rice,
between airport dreams
and Google Maps pins.

And one day,
when we do go—
I'll find you again
in a place we've never been
but always belonged.

18. Who's Gonna Do Stuff With Me

Who's gonna send me those reels at 2 a.m.
that feel like inside jokes with no setup,
like you knew the exact second I'd smile,
before I even opened them?

Who's gonna pick out a spoon
in Home Centre
and say, *"This one's for our future kitchen,"*
with that stupid serious face?

Who's gonna remind me
how to hold chopsticks properly—
then steal my sushi
the moment I get it right?

Who's gonna pause the movie
just to scream about a plot twist
they already saw coming,
then pretend they didn't?

Who's gonna hold my hand
across five FaceTime calls a day,
call me names no one else is allowed to,

and look at me with a cat filter on?

Who's gonna draw a comic
on a dumb little prompt,
and end up telling the same story
I was halfway through?

Who's gonna laugh with me
at Shinchan for the hundredth time,
then say we should really go
to Kasukabe someday?

Who's gonna play Spider-Man
in that café with the burnt-edge crust,
while I sit beside them, watching,
pretending not to fall harder with each swing?

Who's gonna be the voice
I can hear without hearing,
the person I can text
without checking the phone?

And who, honestly—
who's gonna do all the stupid,
tiny, wonderful things
that never mattered
until they weren't with you?

It's not just about missing you.
It's not even just the big things—
not the trips we didn't take,
or the dreams we half-built
before the world changed shape.

It's the small, stupid stuff.
It's not knowing who to send that meme to.
It's opening an app
and realizing there's no one waiting.
It's watching something funny
and laughing for a second too long,
because no one's laughing with me.

It's not having anyone
to narrate my day to.
It's saying things out loud
to an empty room,
just to pretend you're still on the other end.

It's sitting with a thought,
and instead of sharing it,
just... letting it die.

It's not just missing you.
It's missing the rhythm of us.

The background hum of being known.
The way even silence had your shape in it.
The way nothing now
feels like it's meant to be shared.

19. What Love Might Be

Love is the silence that doesn't feel wrong,
The pause in the chaos that still feels strong.
It's coffee half-spilled on a lazy day bed,
It's laughing at nothing, then all that's unsaid.

It's showing up raw when your guard isn't tight,
It's saying you're fine, but they still know it's not right.
It's words that get stuck, but they don't walk away—
It's knowing they're staying, with nothing to say.

It's crying in bed with your back to the wall,
It's someone who hears you before you call.
It's not being perfect to earn their care,
It's knowing, somehow, they'll still be there.

It's laughing at things no one else would get,
It's fights that don't end in anger or threat.
It's honesty clumsy, and timing all wrong—
But something inside says, this still belongs.

It's reaching for touch when your chest feels numb,
It's staying through nights when the feelings don't come.
It's thinking of leaving, but choosing to stay,
Not knowing the words, but showing up anyway.

It's not from a thread or a late-night reel,
It's not what you say—it's what you feel.
It's not from a theory or self-help guide,
It's found when your guard drops, and you don't hide.

It's awkward. It's quiet. It's not always smooth.
It's two people learning what they never proved.
It's trust that is built, not just understood,
It's fucking things up, and still being good.

It's not something earned by getting things right,
It's what wraps around you on your worst night.
It's messy, uncertain, not always serene—
But somehow, in all of it, you feel seen.

20. If It's You

I still wait like I used to do,
Staring at my phone for you.
Every buzz — a rising tide,
Hope and silence side by side.

I wake at three with heartbeats loud,
Half-asleep, half somehow proud.
Your name still floats on dim-lit screens,
Then fades like smoke between my dreams.

I scroll through chats I've read before,
Each word a ghost I can't ignore.
The way you typed, the way you'd tease,
Now echo back in quiet freeze.

Some mornings I forget you're gone,
And reach for you like nothing's wrong.
My pillow folds the way you curled,
And I fall back into that world.

I see your face in passing trains,
In window glass, in bursts of rain.
It isn't you, but still I stare—
Some part of me thinks you'll be there.

I say your name when no one's near,
As if the air might make you hear..
And though I know it isn't fair,
I check my phone like you'd be there.

21. A Galaxy Made For Two

We didn't just fall in love —
We crash-landed, hyperspeed above.
Lightsabers drawn, snacks in hand,
Star Wars nights were where we'd land.

From Clone Wars arcs to rebels' cries,
We watched it all through midnight skies.
You'd nap through credits, miss the fight,
Then claim you knew the plot was right.

You gifted books you wouldn't read,
Still said, "These are for your Jedi needs."
I shelved them like a sacred vow—
Still flip through them sometimes now.

You said you were Padmé, proud and wise,
And I, your Anakin with stormcloud eyes.
But I'd call you Jar Jar just to tease,
You'd sigh, "You wish, Kenobi" then mock with ease.

We argued scenes, rewound old lore,
Made super cute paintings and droid decor.
The Force was strong in quiet things—
Cartoon marathons and spicy chicken wings.

If I ever cross the stars alone,
And find twin suns on a world unknown,
I'll smile at those suns and whisper low:
"Hello there... I still miss you so."

www.ingramcontent.com/pod-product-compliance
Lightning Source LLC
Chambersburg PA
CBHW061725130726
47996CB00006B/2500